Published in the United States of America by The Child's World®
PO Box 326 • Chanhassen, MN 55317-0326
800-599-READ • www.childsworld.com

My First Steps to Math™ is a registered trademark of Scholastic, Inc.

Library of Congress Cataloging-in-Publication Data
Moncure, Jane Belk.
My six book / by Jane Belk Moncure.
p. cm. — (My first steps to math)
ISBN 1-59296-661-6 (lib. bdg. : alk. paper)
1. Counting—Juvenile literature. 2. Number concept—Juvenile literature. I. Title.
QA113.M6676 2006
513.2'11—dc22
2005025696

My "six" Book

by Jane Belk Moncure

illustrated by Rusty Fletcher

This is Little six.

Little  lives in the house of six.

It has six rooms. Count them.

Every day, Little  goes for a walk.

One day, she walks in the woods.

She sees three chipmunks on a stump . . .

and three chipmunks under a tree. Count them.

"We are looking for nuts and seeds," they say.

"I will help you," says Little  .

She finds four nuts on the ground.

She finds two nuts under a log.

Does she have a nut for each chipmunk? Count the nuts.

A mama fox appears. Little 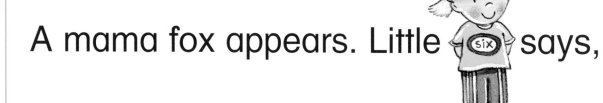 says,

"Run and hide, chipmunks."

How many run down a hole?

Then five little foxes come looking for their mama. How many foxes are there?

Little  says, "Go home, foxes."

Then Little six sees . . .

two big robins
near a nest.

She peeks in the nest and counts four baby robins.

How many robins are there?

Little  sees some toads in the grass.

How many toads does she see?

Little  jumps over the first toad.

How many toads jump away
and hide behind a rock?

Little  is tired.

She sits down in the grass.
Guess what?

Four grasshoppers jump up!

Then two more grasshoppers jump up.

Little jumps up, too.

She jumps six jumps. Can you?

Then Little  sits down again. One of the grasshoppers jumps into her hand.

She counts its legs. How many are there?

"You have more legs than I have," she says. How many more?

The grasshopper is sad. So she lets it go.

How many happy grasshoppers hop away?

Little  sees that it is getting dark.
She hears, *Whoo, whoo.*

How many owls does she see
in the tree?

Then she hears, *Whoo!*
Whoo!
Whoo!
Whoo!

How many little owls peek out of a hole in the tree?

Little six says, "Who-o are you?"

How many big owls
fly into the hole?

Little looks up
at the night sky.

What does she see?

Brightly shining stars!

Little  counts them.
How many?

"I will make six wishes," she says.

Her first wish is for a birthday cake.

Her second wish is for six candles.

Her third wish is for lots of friends like you.

"I will give my last three wishes to you!" she says.

What will your wishes be?

Little 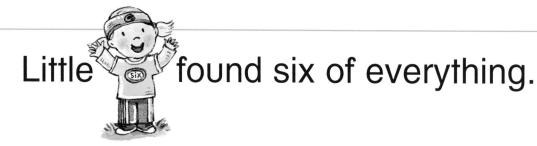 found six of everything.

six chipmunks

six foxes

six robins

six grasshoppers

six toads

six owls

Now you find six things.

Let's add with Little .

 +  =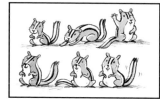

6 + 0 = 6

 +  =

3 + 3 = 6

Now take away.

6   –   1   =   5

6   –   0   =   6

Little 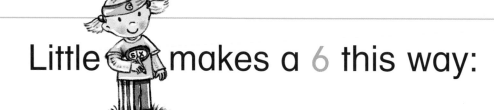 makes a 6 this way:

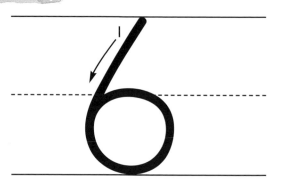

She makes the number word like this:

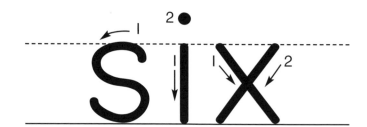

You can make them in the air with your finger.